Tower of Babel

The Biblical Legend of Babylon

Table of Contents

Introduction

The Tower of Babel is a fascinating story, one that has garnered a lot of attention to date and becomes a topic of great controversy among historians and biblical scholars around the world. It is one of the strangest tales mentioned in the Bible that is surrounded by many myths and explanations. In a metaphorical sense, the story of the Tower of Babel expresses the failed attempts of men to gain power, be independent, and establish self-rule. It was also interpreted as a symbol of God oppressing man's pride, and ultimately saving him from self-destruction.

There are several traditional and modern interpretations of the Tower of Babel, some of which even seek to prove its existence in real life. If you're intrigued, this book will tell you the entire story of the Tower of Babel with relevant myths and perceptions.

In essence, this book will walk you through the entire story of the Tower of Babel – how it originated, where it was mentioned, the historical context, related myths, speculations about its construction and composition, the evolution of languages, and finally, how it is perceived in popular culture.

Chapter One:

Historical Context

The first instance of the Tower of Babel was mentioned in Genesis 11 within the first 9 verses. According to the biblical text, all people existing on the face of the Earth were unified and spoke the same language. In time, they all moved East and discovered a plain in the Shinar region in Babylonia where they settled. They then decided to build a city in which they could collectively establish a community. To that end, they used tar as mortar, and brick as stone, as substitutes for the construction materials. They got together and built one of the most noteworthy cities that they took pride in. The news of this exceptional construction reached far and wide across other regions, and people flocked to Shinar to admire its beauty.

However, the residents felt that visitors would copy their style and build something better. To stay ahead, they decided to build a tower that no one could ever match or compete against. The leader of their group imagined building a tower that could touch the sky and reach heaven. All members of the community agreed, and they started the project. Naturally, it took many years until this magnificent tower project saw the light of day.

It is also believed that by building this tower, the people on Earth wanted to divide heaven and Earth as separate domains. Earth would be man's domain, and heaven would be God's domain. In doing so, they were also developing a name for themselves. This would prevent them from being scattered across the Earth. God wasn't happy with this construction; He claimed that by erecting this tower and the city, people on Earth had changed and became proud. Because of their skills and a new city, they did not want God's help anymore. To overcome this, God decided to visit Earth and take action. By confusing them through a change of language, men would no longer be able to communicate and coordinate to see their project through.

According to Genesis 6, the Sons of God visited Earth because they noticed how beautiful the daughters of these men were. This caused a conflict between men and God, resulting in the 'Earth and heaven division.' In parallel, it is also believed that Satan, who was once in heaven, came down to Earth and blatantly violated the division between Earth and heaven. Because of this incident, the Tower of Babel was allegedly built so that it could pierce this line of division. After the tower was built, God visited Earth and witnessed the construction of this structure. This instance is mentioned in Genesis 11, verse 5.

Once he saw the tower, God proclaimed that all people on Earth are one and share one common language. With this, all men shall have the power to do whatever they desire. They had already undertaken this construction, and this is what they continued to do.

In light of this, God decided to cause confusion by scattering men across the face of the Earth. In addition, they would be unable to understand each other's language. Everyone spoke a different tongue and uttered different words, which caused turmoil and chaos. Due to this fear and their inability to understand each other, men stopped constructing and expanding the city as it was intended. This was when it came to be known as Babel. Eventually, all men were dispersed across the Earth, no longer sharing a common, unique language. They did so because they realized that they could no longer live in harmony.

Therefore, men moved across to the eastern part of Earth, settled in a region, and began building a city and a tower. Because of the heaven-Earth divide, they wanted to build the tower so high that it could pierce the divine separation. With this, God came down to the Earth, scattered all men, and changed their language. We can infer from this that men wanted to build their own city and make a name for themselves.

This act of rebellion mentioned in Genesis 11 also states that men were tired of being "named." They wanted to establish an identity, which would become their own. Their ultimate goal was to find happiness and be independent. This independence and autonomy could only be found if they changed their names and were recognized for what they were striving for. However, by crafting their own name and recognition, they did not want to become popular. Instead, they simply wished to conduct their lives on their own terms and dictate their own independent rules. With their own city, they could declare their own laws, rule over the land, and grow their power.

Apart from a new set of rules and rights, men also wanted to build their own institutions within the city, such as corporations and government bodies. After creating these entities, they would be given their own rights, making men the most powerful of all. In other words, men would be all-powerful only in their own city. It was also noted that men were growing tired of this separation from God and thus wanted to reverse God's orders. Instead of being scattered across the face of the Earth, they wanted to stay united. As the Bible recounts, God told Adam to be fruitful and multiply. With this, men would fill the Earth and give rise to a massive population. Similarly, Noah was given the same command by God - to multiply and inhabit the Earth.

It is witnessed in the story of Babel that men did not want to breed and fill the Earth. Rather, they wanted to stay together, build a city, and impose self-power. God, wary of this situation, came down to Earth to take matters into his own hands. God's first remedial move was to confuse the tongue of all men and disrupt their integration to stop them from building and residing in one city. In another instance, the day of Pentecost shows a reversed order. All men gathered in the upper room to speak in all languages, particularly the disciples and Apostles. The people surrounding these men could understand what they were saying and able to follow along. The power of the Holy Church and the Holy Spirit is believed to have made this possible. It is also alleged that the modern men wished to finish the construction of the Tower of Babel and take power and control of the global government, global unity, and global economy.

Construction of New Cities

After Cain developed a city and men attempted to construct a town around the Tower of Babel, God took different actions (Genesis, chapter 12). Abram, a pagan living in a pagan world in the eastern part of Earth, was commanded by God to come out of the city. He was asked to leave his country and make his way to a new city. God intended to build a new city, and Abram was expected to go to that town, known as New Jerusalem. By then, Satan knew of God's intentions and why he created human beings. Also, he was aware of the weaknesses of all humans and why God put together this plan. To counter God's intentions, Satan was constantly ripping off his plans and getting in his way. To combat this situation, God built the new sacred city of New Jerusalem for the men of the earth.

Cain also desired a city, but according to God, his choice of city was completely wrong. In contrast, Abram wanted to live in a city that was made by God. Even though it was a city that Abram couldn't see, he was motivated by it. So, in an attempt to counterfeit God's plan, Satan created a city that was so alluring that all men couldn't deny it. According to them, the desire to live in and establish this counterfeit city was not wrong as God wanted to provide them a new city, anyway. It is believed that the cities we have today are forgeries, perverted versions of the city of New Jerusalem, the city that God wanted us to have.

When the Israelis first started building their city, God called Moses at the back of a desert. After having spent some time there, God asked him to go back to the city and bring all his people out. Now, the chosen people built the first city for their King Pharaoh at the time of their bondage in Egypt. While they were building the city, they also come across slavery in the city of man. A large portion of God's slavery, in fact, went into building this city in Egypt. Upon learning so many values and skills in Egypt, these Israelites polluted the other cities with their new values. This would then be caught on in Israel. When the first city was built, it established a foundation for learning, skills, and values, which would then be passed on to other cities of Israel. Upon knowing the concept of slavery, the Egyptians hired taskmasters to manage them and afflict them with labor.

It is also believed that the city of Manas was made by men and not by God. Every creation that is strictly confined to or glorifies men isn't appreciated and respected by God. This is because every place built by men for self-reliance and power represents and opposition to God and his divine action. By building his own city, a man isn't respecting the presence of God; as such, these cities will not last into eternity. Now, by settling in the city, a man stops his wandering quest and begins to feel secure, grounded, and relieved. He feels that by settling in a city, he can finally experience a sense of community and happiness. He can also hide within the city.

Nevertheless, he overlooks one crucial aspect. Aside from a sense of security and community, the city in which he settles or desires to settle also offers him slavery. And with slavery, a man is deprived of freedom. However, he is alluded by the city as it is a symbol of his triumph and creation that he built with his own mind and hands.

As the Bible says, "all cities will fall in a moment," which illustrates this last point. However, a man is still resilient and keeps building city after city without halting. He wants to gain and exercise limitless power, which makes him greedy and insatiable for erecting new towns. By building and residing in a city, he convinces himself that he is a king, and denies reality. In reality, he is merely but a slave in the city.

Chapter Two:

Myths

As mentioned, several myths are surrounding the Tower of Babel. While some historical sources connect the existence of the tower to other notable structures, other mythical records and bellies relate the tower's tale to its initial Biblical narrative.

Mexico

Mexico, among and other parts of Central America, share the same traditions and beliefs as the original tale of the Tower of Babel. After the conquest of Mexico ended in the early 16th century, the Dominican friar Diego Durán was in Cholula when he met with a 100-year old priest. Among a plethora of fascinating stories and comparisons, the priest told Diego about the Great Pyramid of Cholula. In some Central American traditions, it is believed that the Tower of Babel was somehow or entirely connected to the Great Pyramid of Cholula. According to the priest's story, when sunlight first spread on the face of the Earth, giants appeared and began their quest for the sun. Their initial search was unsuccessful, leading them to build a tower that reached the sky. With this, they could search for the sun. However, this infuriated God and prompted him to order the scattering of the inhabitants on Earth. In the end, the tower was destroyed, too.

Now, unlike other stories that mention the change in languages and flooding on Earth after God's commandment, Mexican myths talk about how the giants were scattered and place great emphasis on the construction of the tower itself. This can be witnessed in the sincere work of connection put forward by Frazer.

The ancient Toltecs were told another story by native historian Fernando de Alva Cortés Ixtlilxóchitl. In line with his beliefs, men suffered harsh repercussions after going through a painstaking deluge. After that, they bred and multiplied in number. To prevent another deluge and the consequent suffering, they built a "zacauli," a kind of tall tower that would protect them. This was ended when all men separated and moved to the other regions of the world.

The Mexican and Central American historical tradition validates the belief that the Tower of Babel was similar to the Great Pyramid of Cholula. It also says the structure was built by giants in search of the sun or men who wanted to protect themselves from another deluge. In the end, the languages changed, and men scattered, just like the traditional tale of the Tower of Babel.

Sumerian Myth

According to the Sumerian myth, also popularly known as the Enmerkar and the Lord of Aratta, a giant ziggurat wished to build in the region of Eridu by Uruk's Enmerkar. To complete his construction project, Enmerkar ordered the import of several precious metals from Aratta. Several requests and an incantation took place to bring back the linguistic commonality, which was made in favor of the God Enki. Some inhabited places in the region, such as Hamazi, Sumer, Shubur, Uri-ki (Akkad), and the Martu land, spoke different languages, a natural distinction that needed to be changed. So, to restore the normal order, they wanted the inhabitants of the Earth and the whole universe to address Enlil in a common language. Also, during the 8th century, at the time of the Neo-Assyrian Empire, an Assyrian myth spoke of a similar tale surrounding the Tower of Babel, which bears multiple similarities to the story mentioned in the Bible.

Among other myths, traditions, and beliefs, the Sumerian and Assyrian myths shared several points of resemblance to the biblical tale of the Tower of Babel.

Other Myths and Traditions

Alongside these two, several other countries and regions still believe in this or a similar story, so much so that they are deeply rooted within their cultural and religious beliefs up until today.

- **Botswana:** In 1849, David Livingstone, a physician, and Christian missionary, met a group of people residing near Lake Ngami and who allegedly shared a similar tradition.
- **Nepal:** It is known that the Tharu in Nepal and other parts of Northern India still believe in a similar legend.

- **Arizona:** The beliefs shared by the Tohono O'odham people in Arizona aren't entirely similar to the biblical tale. In fact, it mainly revolves around Montezuma, the heroic God who was significant among the Amerindian tribes of the Southwest United States, with the Tohono O'odham and Pueblo tribes being the most prominent. So, according to the myth, Montezuma was in the midst of a devastating flood, which he escaped with great fortune and an act of bravery. After this incident, he grew evil and wicked and intended to reach heaven. He then set out to build a horse that would take him to the sky. However, Lord was furious, and his horse was reduced to ashes with thunderbolts.
- **Lozi Mythology:** Sir James George Frazer, a Scottish social anthropologist, wrote a book in 1918 entitled "Folklore in the Old Testament." In his book, Frazer stated some of the most notable Old Testament stories, such as the indigenous legends and the Flood that occurred during these times. He also studied the Botswana incident that was experi-

enced by David Livingstone. He found out that this incident was majorly connected to or shared similarities with some records and tales in Lozi mythology. According to the latter, men wanted to pursue their God, Nyambe, who was believed to have fled on a spider-web and settled in Heaven. The wicked men wanted to see their God, which is why they built a tower of masts to reach heaven. Furious with their actions, God destroyed the masts, and the men perished. In his book, Frazer also infers how the tale of Ashanti is similar to the tale found in Lozi mythology. The only notable difference is that the masts are replaced by a pile of porridge pestles.

- **Karen People of Myanmar:** The Karen people of Myanmar were also studied by Frazer. According to him, the Karen people were directly influenced by the Abrahamic tale and that their origin was actually deemed to be the land of the Karenni, located farther away. Their ancestors, some thirty generations traced back from Adam, built a great pagoda in their original land, after which they were separated by language. This led to the split between Karen and Karenni. The great pagoda mentioned here can be seen as a mirror to the construction of the Tower of Babel.

- **Kongo People**: The Kongo people and the inhabitants of Tanzania also shared a similar myth. In their tradition, they stack a pile of trees or poles to reach the moon. Nonetheless, their attempt turned out to be a gross failure. The Karbi and Kuki people of Assam, some of the oldest tribes in the region, also shared a similar belief.
- **Admiralty Islands:** Lastly, the original tales in the Admiralty Islands (Alaska) also shared a similar tale. According to historical sources, their ancestors tried to build several houses that could reach heaven. However, their attempts failed, and their languages changed at the end.

We have seen numerous stories, beliefs, and interpretations of the Tower of Babel. Now, is there any proof of its actual existence? How is its existence perceived in today's world?

Did the Tower of Babel Really Exist?

While some people believe that the Tower of Babel was a legend and a symbolic representation in folklore, others believe that this tower did actually exist. Several modern studies and findings offer proof of the same. Jeff Allen, from the World Monuments Fund, claims that the Tower of Babel actually existed. The legendary town of Babylon, which can be found today in Iraq, still harbors some fragile vestiges from the past. A significant and vast patch of remains was recognized as the Tower of Babel, which was also backed up by ancient records.

Furthermore, historians who studied the records have corroborated the plausible construction and structure of the tower. In addition, recent findings have shed some light on the existence of the tower. Stones or tablets excavated from Babylon around a century ago, when joined together, produce an etching of the tower's shape on its surface. It is speculated that this entire tablet dates back to the 6th century BC, and there were no previous records. The tablet was owned by private entities, which made it quite difficult for the linguists to study. This would explain why there was no concrete evidence as of yet.

This drawing was studied by Dr. Andrew George, an expert in ancient texts and historical studies. He was successful in bringing the carvings back to life and deciphering a plausible pattern that could be the silhouette of the tower. The top part of the tablet represents a relief that depicts a stepped tower. The left part shows a human being carrying a weapon or a tool with a strange hat or a protective headset. The lower part of the tablet carries some text that is chiseled on the surface. According to George, the text is easy to recognize, and translates to "temple tower of the city of Babylon." This image extracted from the tablet represents a stepped tower with the actual shape of its structure. This study also claimed that the structure was a Mesopotamian stepped tower. The entire structure is divided into seven tiers, as represented in the illustration on the tablet. The depiction of the human being on the other side of the tablet is deemed to be Nebuchadnezzar II, King of the Neo-Babylonian Empire around 600 BC, who was Mesopotamia's most influential ruler. George also believes that the tower was built by this Babylonian ruler.

Interestingly enough, the chiseled texts further reveal the construction type and details about the structure and how the ruler commanded his men to build it. The text reads from the upper sea, which is the Mediterranean to the lower sea, or the Persian Gulf. The people within these regions were mobilized to help complete the construction of the tower.

In contrast, several biblical historians and researchers contradict Andrew George's findings. One such scholar, Bodie Hodge, who works with Answers in Genesis as a researcher, does agree with the proof of the tower's existence and that it dates back to 600 BC. However, he believes that both the Smithsonian channel (on which Andrew George displayed his findings) was slightly mistaken. He claims that the tower wasn't built by Nebuchadnezzar II as it was more than 900 years old, preceding Nebuchadnezzar II's rule. It is plausible that this ancient King might have ordered repairs on the tower, but it is nearly impossible that he was responsible for its construction.

Chapter Three:

Construction and Composition

The construction and architecture of the tower remain fairly vague. As we know, through the Biblical tale, brick and mortar were used as materials for the construction of the tower. With inferences from ancient tales and a detailed study by many historians, several paintings and plausible images have resurfaced to date. One of the most noteworthy appearances of the Tower of Babel is witnessed in the Latin book 'Turris Babel,' which was written by Athanasius Kircher in 1679. The picture of the tower was illustrated by Lieven Cruyl and etched by Coenraet Decker. It is one of the most impressive depictions of the tower due to the minute details and an interesting architecture foreclosure.

This depiction was traced from the original Biblical story and reformed into a probable image. The artist's imagination helps us understand what the tower might have looked like.

According to the tale, the tower was a tall structure that was intended to reach heaven. This is why the tower can be seen as going above the clouds. It still gives an incomplete structural model as God interrupted the construction by changing the builders' language. This is also supported by scaffolding depicted on top of the tower. That was meant for the consolidation and continuation of the construction process. Throughout the structure, decorative elements and supporting arches are evident. The depiction in Genesis 11:3 reports that kilns were built around the tower, shaped in the form of igloos, and used to fire bricks for structural strength and stability. The ramps look like highways followed by constructors to climb the tower and transport building materials to the top with ease.

Image source: https://biblescienceguy.wordpress.com/2013/03/20/3-tower-of-babel-what-did-it-look-like/

On the upper ramps, housing structures can be noticed on the edges. These seem like penthouses constructed either for the King or the wealthy people of that era. In the tower's periphery, several sailing ships are seen, some of which bear dragon heads on the prows. Also, the objects in the tower's context intriguingly represent the tower's huge proportions and massive scale. The background shows pyramids, municipal centers, and some of the most importing towers ever built, which appear tiny next to the gigantic tower.

The depiction of this tower is further supported by the old and new archaeological findings discovered on the site. This architectural feat grew to such popularity that many students and aspiring architects still take this structure as a significant study project. According to Greek historian Herodotus (c. 484 to 425 BC), the tower stood tall with twenty stories and eight levels when he claimed to have seen it during his visit to Babylon.

Chapter Four:

Evolution and Languages

As we know, men shared a common language in the past. To impede the construction of cities and the tower, God dispersed all men across the face of Earth and imposed a series of different languages. It is believed that major language groups find their origin as a result of this divine intervention. Pseudo-linguistics is the term coined to explain the belief that modern languages were extracted and interpreted from the incident of the Tower of Babel. It imposes major contractions on the other evidence for the evolution of languages.

How Did Languages Multiply?

Genesis 11:1, which describes the introduction of the Tower of Babel, also says that, during that time, people shared a common language. However, in a slightly varying account in Genesis 10:5, people were admittedly already separated into several nations. They spoke different languages after the descendants of Ham, Shem, and Japheth segregated the people under their rule. Each nation spoke their own tongue, followed their own rules, and lived in peace and harmony under their own borders. The origin of the common language premise is also backed up by several mythical accounts across cultures and nations. According to these, everyone shared one language that was dedicated to mankind, which was then divided into several after facing God's wrath. That said, not all accounts share the story of the tower's existence.

In Greek mythology, it is said that Hermes, the herald of Gods and humans, thieves, orators, and merchants, was responsible for confusing all languages, giving birth to multiple dialects. This caused Zeus to give up his throne and pass it on to Phoroneus. This tale is often compared to a story mentioned in "the Cooking of Languages," which is an old Estonian myth from northeastern Europe. A similar story is upheld in many other parts of the world such as among the Kacha Naga tribe of Assam, the Maidu people of California, the Wasania people of Kenya, the Tlingit people of Alaska, people settled in the Encounter Bay of Australia, or the K'iche' Maya people of Guatemala.

The Relation Between Science and Myth in the Evolution of Languages

In a very compelling explanation, Professor Steve Jones, a British geneticist, compared the virtue of evolution to the belief of the existence of the Tower of Babel. According to him, Darwin simplistically described the concept of evolution, with just three words, which were "descent with modification." When one generation descends from the previous one, they carry certain modifications in their DNA, which could be mistakes or even mutations. They are plausible errors built up during this passing of information from one generation to the next. However, there is another process, a more successful one, perhaps, which is natural selection. Here, the passing of information is defined as a series of more successful mistakes rather than errors. In scientific terms, evolution is plainly genetics combined with time or a biological descent with a set of modifications (both successful and unsuccessful).

Now, this term 'evolution' can be further demonstrated by connecting it to the ancient Biblical story of the Tower of Babel, and a relevant belief of the evolution of languages. As we know by far, God separated all tongues to make communication impossible among all men, which eventually led to confusion and segregation of habitats. Ironically enough, however, as Professor Jones claims, the existence of language is one of the initial proofs for the existence of the evolution process. This was initially argued by William Jones, a philologist and puisne judge in 18th century Bengal, and who was schooled at Harrow. At Harrow school, Jones took a legitimate interest in various languages and soon became a linguistic prodigy. He was fluent in multiple languages, including Welsh, English, Greek, Latin, Hebrew, Arabic, Persian, and had acquired some basics in Chinese. By his 20s, he also got a grasp on major European languages until he was sent to India as a merchant, where he began studying major Indian languages as well. Among all Indian languages, he was chiefly interested in Sanskrit, which served as the basis for many other languages.

Upon studying several languages, William Jones found many striking similarities between Greek, Latin, Sanskrit, and English. Once he had established all the similarities between these languages, it was evident that they all originated from a common ancestor. He further studied these analogies and came up with a language evolution tree, whose branches signified the similarities and evolution of various languages. The chart depicted the connections between Latin, Greek, Sanskrit, Old Irish, Gothic, and Eskimo languages. Out of these, Latin was further divided into the modern Romance language group and included Spanish, Italian, French, Portuguese, and Catalan languages.

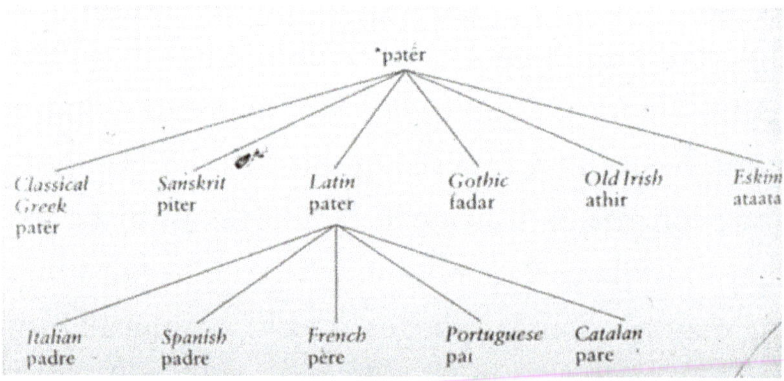

Image source: https://www.youtube.com/watch?v=FW7fJAFC8Mo (Min. 4:07)

Jones believed that if this effort was perpetuated, the extinct word in this tree (which existed even before Latin, Sanskrit, and Greek) could be retracted. In this chart, the common word means 'father,' which has taken several other forms in the language branches. In modern times, this word is denoted as 'PIE' for the Proto-Indo-European language.

It is believed that the original PIE language belonged to the first farmers. This group of languages is believed to be as old as 1,000 to 8,000 years old. The oldest among these is called the Anatolian language, followed by Tocharian, Armenian, Greek, Albanian, Indo-Iranian, Balto-Slavic, Germanic, Italic, and Celtic. Now, these farmers who originally lived in harmony within a common land moved to other regions and took their own languages with them. They taught their respective languages to their children with great accuracy. As they grew up, these offspring added their own nuances and modifications to their languages, which led to major changes over the centuries. As one can expect, the languages we speak today are majorly different from that of our ancestors. This has also led to the extinction of a few languages. Even though

Sanskrit was the most widely known language in ancient India, it is now nearly extinct, spoken by a mere 25,000 as their native tongue.

This also draws a parallel between the tale of the Tower of Babel, and how the farmers spread across various regions, scattering their languages in the process.

Significance and Contradiction of Languages

Genesis 10:5 tells a rather contradicting story. According to the Biblical record, major descendants were born with a different tongue, most notably the descendants of Gomer, Japheth, and Javan. This prompted several speculative theories and debates, some of which continue to date. At one point during the Middle Ages, it was believed that God used the Hebrew language to talk to and address Adam in Paradise. This belief was widespread by most of the Muslim, Jewish, and Christian faith scholars and philosophers. Some records also suggest that Adam used the 'Adamic' language. Scholars and other significant figures argued that the Adamic language was unmodifiable due to its significance. One of those influential figures was Dante Alighieri, who discusses this theory in his "De vulgari eloquentia." Concomitantly, he mentions that Eve addressed the serpent in the first speech act instead of addressing Adam.

This point is slightly tweaked in his Divine Comedy. In this record, Alighieri contends that the Adamic language emerged from Adam himself, and can be solely be attributed as his product. With this, the language could no longer be considered as immutable. This led him to a major realization, namely that the Hebrew language could no longer be deemed as the exclusive language of Paradise. Furthermore, his conclusion supports that the Hebrew language derived from Adam. As God is known as El in his chief Hebrew name, it was speculated that the name would have been derived from a different Adamic version. Alighieri also claimed that Hebrew was derived from the Adamic language, which partly implies the derivation of the name 'El.'

Jewish writers from that period also sought to study the origin of the Adamic language and its close relation with today's widely spoken languages. They wanted to find out the 'original' Adamic language, along with the number of languages it was split into. There was a constant debate between the numbers 70 and 72. In another instance, a Persian scholar claimed that the Adamic language was, in fact, Syriac, an Aramaic dialect and primary literary reference between the 4th and 8th centuries in Mesopotamia.

One of the most noteworthy authors, Rasmus Rask, along with a few others, considered these languages to be "Japhetite." This occurred before the Indo-European languages were accepted. As established, the Hebrew language persisted since the beginning as the people who spoke it never fully took part in the construction of the Tower of Babel. This preserved the Hebrew language, which is why it was prioritized over other Japhetic languages. In addition, the Adamic language had some living descendants, most notably: Tuscan (Giovanni Battista Gelli, 1542, Piero Francesco Giambullari, 1564), Gaelic, Swedish (Olaus Rudbeck, 1675), Dutch (Goropius Becanus, 1569, Abraham Mylius, 1612), and German (Georg Philipp Harsdörffer, 1641, Schottel, 1641).

It is believed that at one point, the European nationalists fought and argued to seize ownership of the Adamic language for their own respective tongues. This historical episode was humorously depicted in a satirical tract written by Swedish physician Andreas Kempe in 1688. In another attempt, Olaus Rudbeck claimed that the Swedish language was the original language of all time and that it was derived from the Adamic language. This attempt was also portrayed in a witty light by Kempe in his scathing parody. In it, he showed God speaking Swedish, Adam speaking Danish, and the serpent speaking French.

Among all the popular authors of the 17th century, Gottfried Hensel and Pierre Besnier defended the primacy of the Hebrew language until linguistics, as a modern field of study, was introduced and developed in the late 18th century. Their notable works include 'A philosophical essay for the reunion of the languages'; 'the art of knowing all by the mastery of one' written in 1675 by Besnier; 'Synopsis Universae Philologiae,' written in 1741 by Hensel; all of which discuss this primacy. While there were constant debates about the emergence of languages and the significance of Hebrew, the 17th century witnessed a continuous quest to search any living descendant of the Adamic language.

After much speculation, the supremacy of the Hebrew tongue remained. Despite the myriad of interpretations and changes in the details of the original story, Hebrew still triumphed as the Adamic language. This was mainly due to the Biblical tale, which initially claimed that Adam spoke Hebrew.

Implications in the 18th and 19th Centuries

By this time, all historians, scholars, linguistics, and debaters came to a single conclusion. There was a common language in a commonplace, which later came to be segregated into multiple tongues across different regions. This was inferred from various tales and myths around the world. However, there was still no concrete conclusion regarding the Adamic language.

In the 1700s and 1800s, trade routes flourished, and people began communicating and traveling freely around the world. They discovered each other's culture and language, encouraging many scholars to study the fascinating linguistic patterns. This is when they first extracted a common pattern between the major languages, which surprised a lot of people and changed their viewpoints on the distinct languages of the world. Some of these languages, such as Arabic and Hebrew, shared phonetic correspondences in many of their words. These words proved the existence of cognates, which refer to the words that evolved among several languages through different means (for instance, "coffee" or "sugar"). When these cognates were compared and the morphological similarities established, a family tree could be traced. In addition, upon tracing the branches of this tree, the common ancestor could be derived. However, in the wild world, this trail of cognates could not help discerning a single proto language.

As we now know, several languages are closely related to each other and belong to the same group. For example, Greek, Sanskrit, English, and Irish belonged to the Indo-European language family. Similarly, the regions spanning from the South China Sea to the Eastern Pacific shared the languages from the Austronesian language group.

Both these language groups shared their own common ancestors. Surprisingly, Hebrew, which was partly considered the Adamic language and the first tongue of mankind, belongs to the Afroasiatic family. An even more stunning aspect that modern linguists found was that Hebrew, given its prime importance as the main language, wasn't well-preserved over the centuries. The relative languages to Hebrew, such as Aramaic and Arabic, kept consonant distinctions, which were surprisingly worn off in the Hebrew language. Like Hebrew, though, almost all languages witnessed major changes over time.

Inferences in Recent Times

All in all, the story of the Tower of Babel helps us establish a major certainty - that we originally shared a common language, and were all dissipated from that point. We can only trace back to several thousands of years, but beyond that, it is impossible to presuppose anything. Historians and linguists found it difficult to trace it back further, which is when the idea of forming a 'superfamily' came into existence. As such, families were established, and parent languages were reconstructed. Similarly, proto languages were compared to derived cognates as further families were branched out, which was established as the superfamily.

By that time, Joseph Greenberg, an American linguist, suggested a new approach. According to this advice, language families needed to be classified first and compared, and then reconstructed. This step of classifying languages is known as 'mass classification,' which includes taking several languages in a given geographical area of study and deciphering the patterns in them. These patterns could be in typology, vocabulary, and the overall comparative structure (such as the number of vowels and basic word order, which pertain to morphology and syntax). After studying several languages, Greenberg came up with several superfamily clusters, which gave way to many controversies. Some of these groups included Turkic, Indo-European, Mongolian, and Japanese, which collectively belonged to the Eurasiatic superfamily. Along with a similar principle, all American languages were grouped into a superfamily called the Amerind family.

In more recent times, another linguist by the name of Merritt Ruhlen put a great deal of effort into reconstructing the groups throughout the 1990s. He took a bunch of languages from all around the world and compared their vocabulary. From this, he could establish 27 proto words. With Ruhlen's attempt, we can witness the 'proto-world,' the parent of all living languages. This photo-world comprised a series of words such as *ku, *tik, *ma, *kuna, and *akwa. After a decade, he went on to study the typology of this proto world. Interestingly, our ancestors constructed and spoke a sentence with a subject, an object, and ending with a verb. The adjectives were put before nouns, and postpositions were used in place of prepositions.

All this instilled great hope in finally finding the long-lost common and original language. However, historical linguists were not entirely convinced; they claimed that the similarities could be mere coincidences, as there was no strong evidence of these proto words being borrowings. Furthermore, the relevance of these cognates was not entirely satisfactory. Historians of language also claimed that Ruhlen's reconstruction pattern was a bit flimsy and did not have a relevant base. This effectively ended the study and reconstruction of mass comparisons.

Chapter Five:

Mentions and Other Sources of the Tower

Apart from the Bible, several other historical sources had a say on the Tower of Babel, some of which serve as stronger evidence of the tower's existence.

Book of Jubilees

The Book of Jubilees is based on the Jewish calendar and relevant religious laws. One of its main subjects includes the character of Moses and its surrounding preface. It also focuses on the events of the Exodus. The book depicts how Jewish culture already had the Ten Commandments in order before they were imprinted on stone by God (according to Exodus 20). In parallel, it also contains that Genesis account. It is believed that Pharisees wrote the Book of Jubilees during the 2nd century BC, likely around 135-105 BC.

The Book of Jubilees is where one of the most detailed accounts of the Tower of Babel can be found. It mentions how the tower was constructed piece by piece and gave great details as to which construction materials were used. What's more, it also mentions other details related to the tower, such as the height of the wall, and other construction elements.

"And they began to build, and in the fourth week they made brick with fire, and the bricks served them for stone, and the clay with which they cemented them together was asphalt which comes out of the sea, and out of the fountains of water in the land of Shinar. And they built it: forty and three years were they building it; its breadth was 203 bricks, and the height [of a brick] was the third of one; its height amounted to 5433 cubits and two palms, and [the extent of one wall was] thirteen stades [and of the other thirty stades]."

Source: Jubilees 10:20–21, Charles' 1913 Translation (https://en.m.wikipedia.org/wiki/Tower_of_Babel)

In Islamic Tradition and Culture

The Tower of Babel hasn't been named in the Quran or anywhere in the Islamic tradition. However, the Quran does represent a similar storyline depicting the tower in a similar stance. In the Egypt of Moses, Haman is commanded by Pharaoh to build a tower out of stone or clay that would reach heaven. He would then climb on the tower and reach heaven to confront the God of Moses. In Sura 2:102, another story talks about Harut and Marut, two angels who taught magic to the Babylonians. While teaching them, they also mention and warn the Babylonians that magic is a sin, and they were simply being tested by faith. This story slyly mentions the name 'Babil' without much prominence. The name is much more evident in the writings of Yaqut (i, 448 f.) and the Lisān al-'Arab [ar] (xiii. 72). Even though these writings don't mention any presence of the tower, they discuss the plain of Babil, how it was named after mankind was swept with the blowing winds over the plain. After reaching the plain, people were assigned different languages by God only to be scattered again.

Popular Muslim theologian al-Tabari wrote the "History of the Prophets and Kings" in the 9th century, in which he mentions that the Mesopotamian King Nimrod, son of Cush, built the Tower and that it was destroyed by God. He also mentions that all humans shared a common language known as Syriac, which was then converted into 72 different languages by God. Similarly, a popular Muslim historian of the 13th century, Abu al-Fida, tells a relatable story of patriarch Eber, an ancestor of Abraham. He was allowed to continue practicing Hebrew, which was his mother tongue. This was because he did not take part in the construction or assembly of the tower.

Author Yahiya Emerick claims that despite mentions of the tower in some of the most significant Islamic writings, the division of humankind with the separation of languages by God is not really prominent in the beliefs of Muslims. He contends that, in fact, God created different nations for humankind to know each other and coexist.

Third Apocalypse of Baruch

One of the most popular pseudepigrapha, the Third Apocalypse of Baruch, mentions the rewards righteous and sinners would receive in their afterlife. Baruch is the disciple of Jeremiah, who described the revelation that he encountered while visiting heaven. This account differs from the Syriac Apocalypse of Baruch.

The group of sinners comprised the people who commanded and built the tower. In this writing, Baruch witnesses two places, the first of which is the resting place of those 'sinners' who built the tower and went against the divine will. In essence, the people who worked together to build the tower were punished by God, an event which is described in the Third chapter of Baruch's experience. Baruch claimed men were so cruel that they wouldn't let a worker woman off during travail. She was ordered to continue making bricks, even after childbirth. She wrapped her child in her apron and carried her baby while laboring. The men and women continued building the tower endlessly, without interruption, until God came down to Earth and hindered construction by changing their languages. They had already built the tower up to a height of 463 cubits (approximately 696 ft, or 212 m). They intended to pierce heaven using a gimlet and witness the material with which it was made (brass, clay, or iron, said Baruch). But in the end, God did not allow this and proceeded to change their language, scattering them across the face of the earth.

Antiquities of the Jews by Flavius Josephus

Flavius Josephus was a Jewish-Roman historian who wrote the famous 'Antiquities of the Jews' in 94 CE. In his account, he mentioned the Tower of Babel, as it was mentioned in the Hebrew Bible. He says that King Nimrod, the Mesopotamian tyrant who manipulated his people to turn against God, was the main character responsible for building the Tower of Babel. He further mentions that Nimrod was the grandson of Ham, son of Noah. Nimrod duped people into believing that they were solely responsible for their own happiness and that it was not God who made them happy. King Nimrod also made several attempts to turn the current government into tyranny for people to sing along. If people were dependent on Nimrod's power, they would have to support him and no longer fear God. This was what the tyrant intended.

Nimrod's attempt was successful to an extent, and he managed to convince others to stop being 'cowards.' With the command and constant supervision of Nimrod, everyone managed to build a strong and high tower. They did not spare any pain and did not stop until they had a solid foundation. It grew higher and thicker in time. This was mainly because of the multiple hands that unified and contributed to building the structure. Since it was extremely thick, the tower's height seemed shorter than it was. The materials used for its construction notably included burnt brick and bitumen mortar, which were the secrets behind its strength. And then, as we know by now, God changed their language to create confusion and tumult. Men could no longer understand each other, and the project of finishing the tower was put to rest for good. The humans then separated from each other as they could no longer live peacefully. And, since the term 'Babel' in Hebrew means confusion, the place was called Babylon, and the tower Babel.

In addition, the Sibyl also recounts a similar tale, which says:

"When all men were of one language, some of them built a high tower, as if they would thereby ascend up to heaven; but the gods sent storms of wind and overthrew the tower, and gave everyone a peculiar language, and for this reason, it was that the city was called Babylon."

Midrash-Rabbinic Literature

There are several accounts concerning the Tower of Babel, its constructors, and the after-situation in Rabbinic literature. A particularly relevant midrash (Jewish interpretation or commentary of Biblical texts) said, "God has no right to choose the upper world for Himself, and to leave the lower world to us; therefore we will build us a tower, with an idol on the top holding a sword, so that it may appear as if it intended to war with God." Also, the construction workers, designers, and builders of the tower were collectively called "the generation of succession."

The account further added that people were not only defying the actions of God but were insulting Abraham as well. The account also mentions men's growing anger with God and how water poured on Earth once every 1,656 years when heaven tottered. They explained that the columns were built to support their setting during the next outpour. Also, it was explained how some people in the group desired to wage war against God. Further instigation came with the belief that the arrows shot in the direction of heaven would return to Earth's ground covered in blood. This triggered others into believing that they needed to fight the inhabitants of heaven.

While several rabbinic sources claim that it was the main act of Nimrod, others suggest that Nimrod had nothing to do with it and that he was separated from this entity. In a completely different account, the story mentions that only a part of the builders was punished and sent to the three parallel dimensions after being converted into semi-demonic creatures. As such, it is believed that the descendants of these creatures now occupy the three parallel dimensions today.

Book of Mormon

The Book of Mormon tells a tale surrounding a man named Jared. Jared, his brother, and his family all lived in the city of Babel, centuries before the Nephites occupied the region. When people gathered to build the tower and angered God, he immediately came down and changed the inhabitants' language. Jared, concerned for the collective fate, asked his brother to pray to God for forgiveness. He pleaded to God not to change the language of their families and friends. Jared and his brother prayed vehemently until God agreed. The divine power said that their language would not be changed, on one condition - Jared, his brother, and their families would have to leave the land and move to another region. God said that they would be directed to a promised land. Upon agreeing, Jared and his family could still understand one another, and they packed to set off for another land.

They embarked with them their animals, seeds, and other belongings. They caught several fish, birds, and swarms of honeybees to survive during their journey. Jared, his brother, and their families traveled for days on end and through the wilderness.

They did not know where to head for, and what to do until God instructed them through the clouds. He directed them to a land of his choice and said that people living on his land had to serve the Lord. Should they refuse to serve and worship him, they would be destroyed. After accepting this condition, Jared and his family reached the Promised Land that was near the sea, which was claimed to be the Valley of Nimrod. They built tents and stayed there for four years. Later, they traveled to the Americas.

According to the Church of Jesus Christ of Latter-day Saints, "although there are many in our day who consider the accounts of the Flood and tower of Babel to be fiction, Latter-day Saints affirm their reality," claiming that the Tower of Babel, was, in fact, a historical reality.

Pseudo-Philo

Pseudo-Philo is essentially the anonymous author of Biblical Antiquities, also popularly titled as "Liber Antiquitatum Biblicarum" (Book of Biblical Antiquities), or "Pseudo-Philo Biblical Antiquities." These records are preserved in multiple Latin manuscripts that were mainly significant between the period of the 11th and 15th centuries CE. It is speculated that the Pseudo-Philo Biblical Antiquities was actually written between the period of mid-1st century CE and the mid-2nd century CE. According to some relevant records, the construction of the building was commanded by three popular rulers of the time; King Nimrod (Prince of the Hamites), Joktan (Prince of the Semites), and Dodanim (Phenech's son and Prince of the Japhetites).

According to sources, some men rebelled during the construction of the tower and refused to bring materials when ordered. Among them, twelve were arrested for refusing the command of bringing bricks to the construction site. The rebellious faction included Abraham, Lot, Nahor, and a few sons of Joktan. Upon arresting his sons, Joktan came to the rescue of these men and saved them from being punished by the other two princes.

Chapter Six:

Popular Culture

Over the years, the Tower of Babel has taken various forms in popular culture internationally. The Biblical tale and narrative of this tower were either adapted or written in its authentic form to be depicted in movies, books, operas, and theatre plays.

Books

Several authors mentioned the tower or wrote about it as the main subject in their books. The most notable ones are:

- British political philosopher Michael Oakeshott wrote a book entitled On History, published in 1983. He took a modern approach to retell the story of the Tower of Babel after studying the tale's interpretations in different cultures. In it, he expresses how humans are willing to sacrifice culture, freedom, and individuality merely for the sake of experiencing pride in achieving grand objects. He also claims that this disdaining human behavior brings ego, greed, and a lack of modesty because of the fascination towards novelty.

- Another British author, A. S. Byatt, published a novel in 1996 named Babel Tower. The main concept of her novel reflects around how every language varies, and whether humans can share a common language. She also implies how humans fail to understand each other despite their capacity for verbal communication.
- Ted Chiang, an American science fiction novelist, wrote a story titled "Tower of Babylon," in which he writes about a miner who is keen on climbing all the way up to the tower. Upon reaching there, he witnesses a vault of heaven.
- Josiah Bancroft, a fantasy novelist, has published a series of books called "The Books of Babel." The fourth and final part of this saga

is expected to be completed and published soon.

Games

Interestingly enough, the Tower of Babel has been portrayed in one of the most noteworthy video games that were developed over the years.

- In one such popular game developed by Ubisoft, "Prince of Persia: The Two Thrones," the last stages of the game portray the Tower of Babel as the setting, where the final fights take place.
- In "Forge of Empires," a web-based strategy game, the Tower of Babel is portrayed as an "available building" that can be claimed by players.

Movies and Theatre

There are a good number of popular movies and theatre representations that were developed around the tale of the Tower of Babel. Some of the most exceptional works include:

- Adam Darius, a popular American choreographer, worked on a multilingual theatrical interpretation in 1993 that was based on the Tower of Babel. It was held at the Institute of Contemporary Arts (ICA) in London.
- In 1927, renowned Austrian-born filmmaker Fritz Lang directed a movie called "Metropolis," which was inspired by the tower's construction process and the plausible designers behind the work. It loosely narrates the lack of communication that could have occurred between the construction workers and the designers of the building. The movie also portrays a difference of opinion and a growing conflict of interest between the designers and workers. While the designers glorify the beauty of the tower, the workers decipher it through oppressive meanings. Moreover, the greedy living conditions of the workers makes them rebel against the designers, resulting in the tower's destruction.

Music

Let us not forget about music. Some of the most popular modern musical works and interpretations around the Tower of Babel include:

- Russian composer Anton Rubinstein developed an opera after getting inspired by the story "Der Turm zu Babel." The opera was quite popular in the late 19th century.
- A popular Italian progressive metal band named Soul Secret wrote and produced a concept album by tweaking the myth's modernized version. They named the album "Babel."

Another popular instance in which the Tower of Babel was portrayed or inspired includes Pieter Brueghel's portrayal of the Colosseum of Rome and the tower in a conical representation. This representation is similar to many Muslim structures that were discovered in the 19th century. One of them was the Minaret of Samarra in Iraq, which was adapted and presented as a geometrical woodcut and stylized depiction of the monument.

Brueghel's 1563 Painting

If you are already familiar with the Tower of Babel story, you must know about one of its most significant modern interpretations in popular culture. It is Brueghel the Elder's 1563 paintings, which is a series of three oil paintings, all portraying the Tower of Babel as the main theme.

Brueghel was known for the religious subjects that he painted in most of his works. He was in Rome when he first painted a miniature of this painting on ivory support. This was the first painting in the series. Unfortunately, it is now lost, and no one has been able to retrieve it to date. After his first attempt at painting the Tower of Babel, he was commissioned by art collector and historian Niclaes Jonghelinck to do so again. This is the main painting in the series and depicts the Tower of Babel in its exquisite glory, represented in great detail and intricacy. The third painting was again a miniature version of the tower that was painted on wood in 1564.

In the main painting, Brueghel has also depicted King Nimrod and his workers alongside the detailed tower. It shows the King and his men observing the workers in action on the construction site. As we know, King Nimrod and his men were not a part of the Biblical story but were specifically portrayed by Brueghel to showcase his pride and sins to all.

He had painted the tower as a high structure standing magnificently on the ground. It was touching the clouds, featuring numerous windows with intricate details on its surface. At first glance, it is difficult to grasp and observe all the things at once, as a lot is going on inside the frame. The construction workers are on the ground and stretch to the top of the tower. Everyone in the painting is performing a different action, such as watering the plants, cooking over a fire, and even drying off their clothes. This was probably meant to show how humongous a project it was to carry on.

It is quite impressive how Brueghel was able to portray the painting in such an intricate fashion, given the minimal amount of information given in the Bible related to the tower's structure and detailed context. He was able to give some meaning and significance to this lesser-known Biblical tale, which can be absorbed by simply looking at his painting. This is the reason why this particular work of his became so famous. The chef-d'oeuvre is now housed at the Kunsthistorisches Museum in Vienna.

Conclusion

The Tower of Babel was partly portrayed as a metaphorical symbol of man's opposition, and partly as a true incident. As we saw, this evidence varies greatly depending on contexts, interpretations, religious, cultural, and literary significance. However, the tower's destruction is not mentioned in any records, especially in the accounts found in Genesis. We can still extract a few instances of the destruction of this tower, which are evident in sources such as Sibylline Oracles (iii. 117–129), the Book of Jubilees (chapter 10 v.18–27), Abydenus (frags. 5 and 6), Cornelius Alexander (frag. 10), and Josephus (Antiquities 1.4.3).

According to most of these sources, the tower was destroyed when God blew it over with strong, aggressive winds. As per the mid-rush, the tower was ravaged partly because it was burnt, and partly because it was swallowed. The top and bottom parts were destroyed, and the middle was left for time itself to destroy. Ultimately, the mythical tale of the Tower of Babel will remain a subject of debate, controversy, and speculation.

References

https://www.youtube.com/watch?v=bGt0VYVx-wDE

https://www.youtube.com/watch?v=Fz3OsK-GR4Z0

https://www1.cbn.com/cbnnews/us/2017/may/new-evidence-bibles-tower-of-babel-was-real

http://www.pieterbruegel.org/tower-of-babel/

http://www.jewishencyclopedia.com/articles/2563-baruch-apocalypse-of-greek

https://www.christianity.com/wiki/bible/what-is-the-book-of-jubilees.html

https://en.m.wikipedia.org/wiki/Tower_of_Babel

https://www.youtube.com/watch?v=aOrXduUK-FaY

https://www.youtube.com/watch?v=FW7fJAFC-8Mo

https://biblescienceguy.wordpress.com/2013/03/20/3-tower-of-babel-what-did-it-look-like/

https://www.youtube.com/watch?v=YS-QNKYYSTw

Milton Keynes UK
Ingram Content Group UK Ltd.
UKHW022105150124
436101UK00005B/101

9 780645 905939